THE

LAST

SEASON

◆

THE
LAST
SEASON

◆

A Winter Treasury

THE
NATURE
COMPANY

BERKELEY, CALIFORNIA

◆

The Nature Company owes its vision to the world's great naturalists: Charles Darwin, Henry David Thoreau, John Muir, David Brower, Rachel Carson, Jacques Cousteau, and many others. Through their inspiration, we are dedicated to providing products and experiences which encourage the joyous observation, understanding, and appreciation of the world of nature. We do not advocate, and will not allow to be sold in our stores, any products which result from the killing of wild animals for trophy purposes. Seashells, butterflies, furs, and mounted animal specimens fall into this category. Our goal is to provide you with products, insights, and experiences which kindle your own sense of wonder and which help you feel good about yourself and the world in which you live.

Designed by Bonnie Smetts
Printed and bound in Italy
Editorial direction by Catherine Kouts
Editing and research by Robert D. San Souci

Published by
The Nature Company
750 Hearst Avenue
Berkeley, California 94710

T HE NATURAL WORLD IN WINTER HOLDS A MULTITUDE OF extraordinary treasures for those who pause to watch and listen. "Summer diversifies," suggests Edwin Way Teale. "Winter simplifies." Winter pares life to its essentials, at once testing the limits of living things and signaling the next stage in the eternal process of vitality and renewal. Writes Annie Dillard, "All that summer conceals, winter reveals."

We have greatly enjoyed discovering and collecting this wide-ranging, unabashedly eclectic assortment of passages from sources both familiar and unexpected. Our heartfelt hope is that you, the reader, will find equal pleasure and inspiration in savoring the subtle hues, vibrant moods, and essential truths of nature's last season.

— THE EDITORS

"In these 'dead months' of December and January the forest lives its own life. It is not asleep as the poets feign. Sleep has entered the forest, has made the deep silence its habitation; but the forest itself is awake, mysterious, omnipresent, a creature seen at last in its naked majesty.... Go to the winter woods: listen there, look, watch, and 'the dead months' will give you a subtler secret than any you have yet found in the forest." —*William Sharp*

REFLECTIONS

IN A WINTER

LIGHT

"In winter we lead a more inward life."

HENRY DAVID THOREAU

FROM LEAF-FALL TO FIRST SNOW WE THINK of the outdoor world, in these latitudes, as a drab and colorless scene, for our eyes are still remembering October and our hearts remember June. But late fall has its own spectrum, of browns and grays and conifer greens. We begin to recognize that narrower spectrum when the snow comes with its sharp accents. Then the browns stand out, separate from the grays, and the greens of pines and hemlocks and spruces come into their own. Even the bronzed grass and the weed stems of the fields reveal new color to the freshly perceptive eye.

Until snow comes, the elms at the roadside loom black against the sky. Against a white background their clean boles are all subtle browns and grays. The old apple tree is only a dark tangle of branches until a shimmering background reveals its winter motley, not one shade of brown but at least a dozen. On the hillside, doubly emphasized by snow and the bold white strokes of the birches, the pasture cedars are a brownish-green, a brown that verges on the ruddy shade of their own bark. And the heads of the leaning birches have a reddish cast, up where their twigs become a brush against the sky.

Look across a meadow, snow-dusted, and the range of tans

and browns and bronzes is amazing. The bronze of the upland grass, the rusty stems of the ever-curving goldenrod, the oat-straw gold, the cornstalk tan, the clean ruddy red, all are there, and even tobacco brown and buckskin tan, in the frosted grass clumps and the bold seed heads. The colors are there; they have not gone. The spectrum may be narrow, but there is infinite variety, once leaf-fall is forgotten and the winter world has its own background.

—Hal Borland, *Borland Country*

U NLESS THE SKY IS HEAVILY CLOUDED THERE IS ALWAYS SOME
light in the winter night—the bluish aura of the moon, the low,
green glow of aurora, the scattered pinpoints of the stars. They
blaze against the clear, black sky and sometimes shine through the
mistiness of the aurora like jewels on the veil of Time. The red and
blue giants gleam pink and azure amid the twinkling whiteness of
their companions, and the planets carry steadily glowing lanterns
along their ancient paths.

The aurora shows a dim light low in the northern sky all year,
but reaches its splendor in winter when dry air and long hours of
darkness make way for its fabulous light. Sometimes it flames red as
the hearth fires of Valhalla or green as the waves that bore the Vikings'
ships. Or its cold-white banners and curtains strengthen into search-
lights that set the birds twittering. Once I saw a squirrel and two
chickadees come looking for breakfast by aurora-light, only to depart
in confusion when the "dawn" faded from the sky.

There was a night when I woke to windows filled with a puls-
ing, unearthly green. Hastily wrapping myself in clothes heavy
enough to defeat the below-zero air, I went out into a night that one
might be more likely to encounter above the Arctic Circle. The wild
green flare lighted my way as I skittered down the hard-packed snow
of the path onto the wind-ruffled drifts that covered the lake ice.

A mile to the north, the Canadian hills crouched low before a cold and flaming glory. Two silver arcs towered above the rolling horizon like a faded double rainbow, a shimmering band of platinum between, a crystal-flecked velvet darkness beneath. Rays of white and rose swayed high above the arcs and the wavering green overhead seemed to come from everywhere. And, in the quiet night, my ears caught the faint swish and rustle, like lightly touching taffeta ribbons, that is the voice of the aurora. . . .

[Finally] the lights in the sky grew dim. The platinum slowly lost its sheen and the lower darkness grew larger and deeper and seemed to come terrifyingly nearer — a black whirlpool, utterly without light and of endless depth. As my eyes tried to penetrate this opening into space, the northern lights faded. Only a faint glow lingered to outline the hills, and the gray distances stretched on and on.

—Helen Hoover, *The Long-Shadowed Forest*

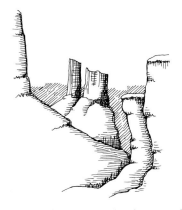

FAR TO THE NORTH, THE GREAT Kaibab plateau, covered with pure white snow and fringed on its edge with the bright green of the stately pines, is sparkling in the morning sun, as if crowned with a diadem of myriads of clearest diamonds and decked with thousands of emerald plumes. To the south and west the vision is bounded by the same high plateaux which lie south and north of the River.

The whole landscape is a network of caverns, gorges, and ravines, and between them are towers, temples, and buttes of every form, dimension, and design.

As the sun rises over the surrounding platform, what a silent, curious change creeps over the whole scene! The clear light of the sun streams through every opening. The eastern walls of the templed buttes burn with almost living flame, while, to the west, are cast long shadows so dark, so bold that they seem as if portions of the night itself had been left behind.

The whole Canyon is still in solemn repose, but, as the sun's light forces its way down, the dark shadows steal away to hide. The inner gorge now wakes from its night of slumber. As shadow chases shadow, and the bright sunlight leaps first here and then there, now around a buttressed point, then into some deep alcove, the whole scene is a moving panorama, of light and shade and mingled tints of celestial beauty.

From beneath the snow-capped summits the gray and yellow of the highest ledges gradually sink, as the eye descends, into a pale, purplish hue, which suddenly flashes out into the fiery scarlet of the middle sandstones. Across the gray talus at their base, the brighter scarlet blends into the rich, deep red of the marble cliffs, and this, gradually melting away, mingling with the purples and darker browns of the lower sandstones, rests for a base upon the black granite of the inner gorge.

Across the chasm to the southwest, into which the sun now pours in all his glory, the noble amphitheaters are opening up their many-colored galleries to view. . . . The vast ensemble so grand, so bold, so wild, and yet grouped together with such symmetry, over all whose outer and inner walls are hung with so much grace those parti-colored draperies in a thousand varied tints, is blended in such harmony that none other than He who first painted the lily and the rose could have been its architect or its painter.

A morning on such a sculptured butte, in the presence of such awful grandeur, while slowly and noiselessly the darkness of night is changed into the beauty and sublimity of a perfect day, is like stand-

ing on some new Mount of Transfiguration, where language fails and
description becomes impossible.

> —John Wesley Powell, *Exploration of the
> Colorado River and Its Tributaries*

I HAD LONG LIVED IN BRIGHT FLOWERY SUMMER, AND I WISHED to see the snow and ice, the divine jewelry of winter once more, and to hear the storm-winds among the trees and rocks, and behold the thin azure of the mountains, and their clouds. . . .

Christmas brought us a cordial, gentle, soothing snowstorm —a thing of plain, palpable, innocent beauty that the frailest child would love. The myriad diamonds of the sky came gracefully in great congregational flakes, not falling or floating, but just coming to their appointed places upon rock or leaf in a loving, living way of their own —snow-gems, flowers of the mountain clouds in whose folds and fields all rivers take their rise. The floral stars of the fields above are planted upon the fields below. The pines, the naked oaks, the bushes, the mosses too and crumpled ferns are all in equal bloom, and belong to the same one great icy order.

—John Muir, *John of the Mountains:*
The Unpublished Journals of John Muir

STANDING QUITE ALONE, FAR IN THE FOREST, while the wind is shaking down snow from the trees, and leaving the only human tracks behind us, we find our reflections of a richer variety than the life of the cities. The chickadee and nuthatch are more inspiring society than statesmen and philosophers, and we shall return to these last as to more vulgar companions. In this lonely glen, with its brook draining the slopes, its creased ice and crystals of all hues, where the spruces and hemlocks stand up on either side, and the rush and sere wild oats in the rivulet itself, our lives are more serene and worthy to contemplate.

— Henry David Thoreau, *A Winter Walk*

T HE COUNTRY IS MORE OF A WILDERNESS, MORE OF A WILD
solitude, in the winter than in the summer. The wild comes
out. The urban, the cultivated, is hidden or negatived. You shall
hardly know a good field from a poor, a meadow from a pasture, a
park from a forest. Lines and boundaries are disregarded; gates and
bar-ways are unclosed; man lets go his hold upon the earth; title-
deeds are deep buried beneath the snow; the best-kept grounds
relapse to a state of nature; under the pressure of the cold, all the
wild creatures become outlaws, and roam abroad beyond their usual
haunts. The partridge comes to the orchard for buds; the rabbit
comes to the garden and lawn; the crows and jays come to the ash-
heap and corn-crib, the snow buntings to the stack and to the barn-
yard; the sparrows pilfer from the domestic fowls; the pine grosbeak
comes down from the north and shears your maples of their buds;
the fox prowls about your premises at night; and the red squirrels
find your grain in the barn or steal the butternuts from your attic. In
fact, winter, like some great calamity, changes the status of most
creatures and sets them adrift. Winter, like poverty, makes us
acquainted with strange bedfellows.

—John Burroughs, *Year in the Fields*

THE BROOK RUSHED AND TINKLED icily, the frozen grasses on the banks of it whispering their brittle winter sound. I made my way to the big willow, near the bend in the brook where the current rushes and swirls among boulders that are patterned by the numberless pebbly cases of caddis worms, and I sat down on the stump and stared at the dark, tumbling water. I stared a long while at it, my thoughts lost in the black speculations that throng a mind when it starts from a miserable mood and then runs idling; and suddenly I noticed, out of the corner of an eye, a little movement of a form amongst the current patterns of the water. It was a muskrat, swimming.

With his small sleek head just above the icy water, the muskrat came paddling upstream toward me. Within a moment or two after I had first seen him, a dozen yards away, he was abreast of me; and now, almost at my feet, he swerved his course and clambered, dripping upon a boulder that I might have touched with my outstretched hand. He sat close beside me now, in the glimmering winter daybreak, and looked at me gravely, unfrightenedly, companionably, and began the preening of his dark, drenched fur.

We sat a long time together, the muskrat and I, and it would be hard to say what thoughts and half-thoughts were born in my mind out of our shared dawn-watching. I thought of the muskrat's life history, perhaps: the way of his birth, in the dark bank burrow, and of his moonlit glidings and divings and fraternizings with his fellows in the secret rush-bordered pools of our creek, and of his browsings among the wet earth-cool bulbs of the wild lilies. Perhaps I did not think at all, except the dim subthought that, in all the muskrat's life on our sanctuary acres, no harm had ever come to him, and that now he thus sat close beside me, no terror in his wild heart. Perhaps, simply, a mood was conveyed to me, more deeply than to the mind. There was renewed in me the ancient insight—call it a kind of prerational faith or call it "deep knowing" as some Algonquian Indians did—that let me feel once more what I had bitterly lost when I began my walk: the old, old peace of earth. Could I say, precisely, what kind of profound inner renewal came to me out of the small adventure of the companionship of a happy muskrat in this morning's bitter dawn, I could say something superbly important. But there isn't any way to get these things said, of course. You can only hint and hope.

—Alan Devoe with Mary Berry Devoe, *Our Animal Neighbors*

IT IS WINTER PROPER; THE COLD weather, such as it is, has come to stay. I bloom indoors in the winter like a forced forsythia; I come in to come out. At night I read and write, and things I have never understood become clear; I reap the harvest of the rest of the year's planting.

Outside, everything has opened up. Winter clear-cuts and reseeds the easy way. Everywhere paths unclog; in late fall and winter, and only then, can I scale the cliff to the Lucas orchard, circle the forested quarry pond, or follow the left-hand bank of Tinker Creek downstream. The woods are acres of sticks; I could walk to the Gulf of Mexico in a straight line. When the leaves fall the striptease is over; things stand mute and revealed. Everywhere skies extend, vistas deepen, walls become windows, doors open.... The mountains' bones poke through, all shoulder and knob and shin. All that summer conceals, winter reveals.

It snowed. It snowed all yesterday and never emptied the sky, although the clouds looked so low and heavy they might drop all at once with a thud. The light is diffuse and hueless, like the light on paper inside a pewter bowl. The snow looks light and the sky dark, but in fact the sky is lighter than the snow. Obviously the thing illuminated cannot be lighter than its illuminator. The classical demonstration of this point involves simply laying a mirror flat on the snow so that it reflects in its surface the sky, and comparing by sight this value to that of snow. This is all very well, even conclusive, but the illusion persists. The dark is overhead and the light at my feet; I'm walking upside-down in the sky.

—Annie Dillard, *Pilgrim at Tinker Creek*

THE FULL MOON OF DECEMBER, WHICH occurred last night, is no summer serenader's moon, no sentimental moon of silvery softness to match the rhyming of the ballad singer. It is a winter's moon with more than fourteen hours of darkness to rule in cold splendor.

It is not a silvery moon at all. This is a moon of ice, cold and distant. But it shimmers the hills where there is a frosting of snow and makes the frozen valleys gleam. It dances on the dark surface of an up-country pond. It glitters in the frost-spangled air over the ice-defying brook. It weaves fantastic patterns on the snow in the woodland. It is the sharp edge of the night wind, the silent feather on the great horned owl's wing, the death-scream of an unwary rabbit when the red fox has made its pounce.

This winter's moon is a silent companion for the night-walker, a deceptive light that challenges the eye. It dims the huddled hemlocks on the hillside, and it sharpens the hilltop horizon. It wreathes the walker's head in the shimmer of his own breath, and it seems to whistle in his footsteps. It makes wreaths of chimney smoke and sweetens the smell of the hearth-fire.

It is the long winter night in cold splendor, night wrapped in frost, spangled and sequined and remote as Arcturus.

—Hal Borland, *Hal Borland's Twelve Moons of the Year*

◆

THE GREAT

WEATHERS

"Blow, blow, thou winter wind!
Thou art not so unkind
As man's ingratitude."

WILLIAM SHAKESPEARE

MY VERMONT NEIGHBORS PAY more than passing attention to a squirrel's tail as winter approaches. It is one means whereby they try to predict the coming season. If the tail looks about as it did during the summer, a mild winter is in the offing. But if it's handsome and thick and nearly as big as its owner, look out: there's a long, cold winter ahead.

The country dweller scrutinizes all manner of signs in an attempt to forecast the winter to come. Along with the condition of the pelts of animals, there is their protective layer of fat. The thicker the fat, the more dramatic the prediction. Lots of fat means a hard winter.

The activity of animals and fish is important, too. If the fishing drops off markedly, it means the fish have left the shallows and retreated to deeper water while there is yet time. An unusual number of dead snakes in the road means they're headed for their dens — another portentous sign. Heavy crops of fruit signal a hard winter, too. And if the bears and chipmunks and woodchucks drop out of sight earlier than usual, it means they probably know something that we don't.

The most famous weather prophet, however, is the woolly bear caterpillar. This larva of the common whitish Isabella moth sports a bristly crew-cut arranged in three bands: black head and forepart, rusty-brown middle, and black tail section. According to my neighbors, the three portions forecast the beginning, middle, and end of winter.

Many caterpillar viewers say that a wide, brown middle means a mild winter with plenty of brown grass and leaves. An abbreviated black forward section means winter will start with a vengeance. And watch out for a caterpillar whose black nether section begins around the middle and continues unabated to the rear of his hurrying little body. This means winter will drag on and on as if it would never end.

And how does the expert—the woolly bear—live up to its own predictions? It simply refuses to enter into the argument at all. Hurrying across the road and into a pile of leaves, it curls up for the winter and goes fast asleep.

—Ronald Rood, *Who Wakes the Groundhog?*

THERE ARE SEVEN OR EIGHT categories of phenomena in the world that are worth talking about, and one of them is the weather. Any time you care to get in your car and drive across the country and over the mountains, come into our valley, cross Tinker Creek, drive up the road to the house, walk across the yard, knock on the door and ask to come in and talk about the weather, you'd be welcome. If you came tonight from up north, you'd have a terrific tailwind; between Tinker and Dead Man you'd chute through the orchardy pass like an iceboat. When I let you in, we might not be able to close the door. The wind shrieks and hisses down the valley, sonant and surd, drying the puddles and dismantling the nests from the trees.

—Annie Dillard, *Pilgrim at Tinker Creek*

THE WONDERFUL PURITY OF NATURE AT this season is a most pleasing fact. Every decayed stump and moss-grown stone and rail, and the dead leaves of autumn, are concealed by a clean napkin of snow. In the bare fields and tinkling woods, see what virtue survives. In the coldest and bleakest places, the warmest charities still maintain a foothold. A cold and searching wind drives away all contagion, and nothing can withstand it but what has a virtue in it, and accordingly, whatever we meet with in cold and bleak places, as the tops of mountains, we respect for a sort of sturdy innocence, a Puritan toughness. All things beside seem to be called in for shelter, and what stays out must be part of the original frame of the universe, and of such valor as God himself. It is invigorating to breathe the cleansed air. Its greater fineness and purity are visible to the eye, and we would fain stay out long and late, that the gales may sigh through us, too, as through the leafless trees, and fit us for the winter—as if we hoped so to borrow some pure and steadfast virtue, which will stead us in all seasons.

—Henry David Thoreau, *A Winter Walk*

I N WINTER, THE WIND IS PREVAILINGLY FROM THE NORTHWEST. The westerlies pile up waves on the other side of the ocean, having had hundreds of miles in which to roll them forward, but on our side, blowing against them from off the land, they iron them out. Under a strong northwester the sea off the beach is ruffled by the wind but at the same time flattened beneath its weight. The low waves seem to slink upon the land, becoming noticeable only at the last minute—and I have never seen a day at the beach with no surf whatever—and they break, a mere foot high, with a sudden, exhausted plop, their crests swept back by the breeze in a white veil of mist.

In the northern, continental weather that the northwester brings, the ocean leads in the mind's eye to the Arctic and the dazzling wall of the glaciers from which icebergs are calved. The air is pure, as sterile as the ether of space, and you feel yourself in an everlasting openness. Poseidon is in another, distant reach of his empire. In the extreme of such conditions, in midwinter when the wind is cruel, the outer beach may be entirely lifeless. You may walk for an hour and see not a gull. Yet there are rewards. You feel better for enduring the knife-edge of winter, and you are privileged to esteem yourself no more fair-weather communicant of the august vastness.

—Charlton Ogburn, Jr., *The Winter Beach*

THE FIRST OF THE GREAT SNOWSTORMS that replenish the Yosemite fountains seldom sets in before the end of November. Then, warned by the sky, wide-awake mountaineers, together with the deer and most of the birds, make haste to the lowlands or foothills; and burrowing marmots, mountain beavers, wood-rats, and other small mountain people, go into winter quarters, some of them not again to see the light of day until the general awakening and resurrection of the spring in June or July. The fertile clouds, drooping and condensing in brooding silence, seem to be thoughtfully examining the forest and streams with reference to the work that lies before them. At length, all their plans perfected, tufted flakes and single starry crystals come in sight, solemnly swirling and glinting to their blessed appointed places; and soon the busy throng fills the sky and makes darkness like night. The first heavy fall is usually from about two to four feet in depth; then with intervals of days or weeks of bright weather storm succeeds storm, heaping snow on snow, until thirty to fifty feet has fallen.

—John Muir, *The Yosemite*

BLIZZARD MUST BE A COINED name; at least, it seems to have no roots in either English or French. The origin of the word is unknown, but its meaning is clear enough. The blizzard is a cyclonic winter storm characterized by high winds, extreme cold, and moderate-to-heavy snowfall.

In northwestern Canada there gathers a pole of intense winter cold, a sort of coalescence of deep frost similar to those in Greenland and Siberia. From this center a wide mantle of heavy, frigid air sinks southward. As it approaches the United States it deflects eastward in a class of winds called "the polar easterlies." When these collide with the warm Gulf and Atlantic air masses that are moving northward into the midcontinent, there is meteorological havoc. Differing greatly in temperature and humidity, and stirred and driven by the polar-front and subtropical jet-streams that encircle the northern hemisphere, these great air masses join in a tempestuous marriage with wild wind systems and unstable atmospheric pressures. The meeting ground of these major air masses is a region of storms and crazy weathers, of major and rapid violent change, and the cyclonic wind systems that spin about centers of low atmospheric pressure in winter to create blizzards covering hundreds of thousands of square miles.

Since its primary component is wind, the classic blizzard is essentially a phenomenon of the open lands — particularly the prairies and plains, where the topography offers little resistance to moving air and the great storms can run almost unimpeded. There may be more snow in northern and eastern forest regions, and certainly as much cold. The difference between winter storms there and the classic prairie blizzard lies in the intensity of unbridled wind that plunges the chill factor to deadly lows, drives a blinding smother of snow during the actual storm, and continues as ground blizzards and white-outs long after snow has stopped falling. Depending on snowfall and wind, the storm may leave drifts three times as tall as a man and is usually followed by calm, silver-blue days of burning cold.

—John Madson, *Where the Sky Began*

R o u g h   W e a t h e r

I HAVE LIVED IN NEBRASKA NOW FOR THIRTY-ODD YEARS AND SO it was no surprise to me that when I had finished taking notes for this collection the fattest stack of cards stood behind the marker labelled "Rough Weather." I cannot imagine that anyone ever gets used to Plains weather. And it is in this category that one really has to sympathize with the honest man, for his dedication to honesty in reporting Plains weather will make him out to be the grossest kind of prevaricator.

A fellow folklorist once asked me why Nebraska barns never have wind vanes. I passed the question on to a seasoned farmer, who replied, "No sense to it. When you want to see which way the wind is blowing, you just look out the window and see which way the barn is leaning."

One farmer, answering my comment about the weather never seeming to be right for farming, said, without humor, "If we didn't have bad weather, we wouldn't have no weather at all."

Stories are rife of soddy dwellers awakening late in the morning to find the room still dark, the windows having been covered with drifted snow. Others tell of the doors of their soddies being blocked by huge drifts, which meant that they had to tunnel out, if the door opened in, or wait for the thaw or dig out through the ceiling if the door opened outward.

[One informant reported:]

"It used to snow so bad that the snow-birds would have to lie on their backs and scratch to keep from being covered up."

[And another:]

"I remember the blizzard of '88 and many other cold winters. Many a time we had to use a ladder to get up on the roof to chop off the smoke clouds that had frozen on the chimney."

And yet another:

"It got so cold in some of the soddies that the fire froze on the candles and they had to bury them to get it dark enough to sleep."

And if that was not trouble enough, in Kansas, once the thaw set in, the flames that townspeople had broken off the candles and lamps and thrown outside thawed out and started minor fires all over town.

"The first thawing days of spring were filled with train whistles and sounds of trains going by, the sounds of which had frozen and thawed out only when warm weather came."

— Roger Welsch, *Shingling the Fog and Other Plains Lies*

WE REACHED ST. PAUL, AT THE head of navigation of the Mississippi, and there our voyage of two thousand miles from New Orleans ended. It is about a ten-day trip by steamer. It can probably be done quicker by rail. I judge so because I know that one may go by rail from St. Louis to Hannibal—a distance of at least a hundred and twenty miles—in seven hours. This is better than walking; unless one is in a hurry.

The season being far advanced when we were in New Orleans, the roses and magnolia blossoms were falling; but here in St. Paul it was the snow. In New Orleans we had caught an occasional withering breath from over a crater, apparently; here in St. Paul we caught a frequent benumbing one from over a glacier, apparently.

I am not trying to astonish by these statistics. No, it is only natural that there should be a sharp difference between climates which lie upon parallels of latitude which are one or two thousand miles apart. I take this position, and will hold it and maintain it in spite of the newspapers. The newspaper thinks it isn't a natural thing; and once a year, in February, it remarks, with ill-concealed exclamation points, that while we, away up here, are fighting snow and ice, folks are having new strawberries and peas down South; callas are blooming out-of-doors, and the people are complaining of the warm weather. The newspaper never gets done being surprised about it.

—Mark Twain, *Life on the Mississippi*

I WATCHED THE MORNINGS TURN PALE GREEN, THEN SAFFRON, then orange, then flame colored while the sky glittered with stars and a sliver of a golden moon hung quietly. I watched a blazing sun vault over a mountain and leave such a path of glory behind that the windows of mountain homes like ours glowed blood red until dark and even the darkness was tinged and wore a cloak of purple instead of the customary deep blue. Every window of our house framed a vista so magnificent that our ruffled curtains were as inappropriate frames as tattered edges on a Van Gogh. In every direction, wherever we went we came to the blue softly curving Sound with its misty horizons, slow passing freighters and fat waddling ferries.

I loved the flat pale blue winter sky that followed a frosty night. I loved the early frosty mornings when the roofs of the chicken houses and the woodshed glowed phosphorescently and the smoke of Bob's pipe trailed along behind him and the windows of the house beamed at me from under their eaves.

Some winter days, [however,] great winds came bounding down out of the north; blew rain at us in spitty gusts; sent the mountain's misty veils flying, exposing their pale haughty faces; crashed around the barn, snapping giant snags and tossing terrible handfuls of limbs just anywhere; grabbed our house by the scruff of its neck and shook it until the windows rattled and the shakes flew off; sniffed

around the eaves of the chicken house hoping for a loose board; then dashed back to annoy the mountains again, prostrating the small trees in its path. It was boisterous and noisy and terrifying.

Bob seemed oblivious of the weather. Apparently lulled by the screaming wind, the falling trees, the lashing rain, he whistled gaily as he pumped up his lanterns and began his evening chores. Bundled in oilskins, lanterns swinging like beacons, feed buckets clanking cheerfully, he walked briskly through the rain. He never even noticed the terrible nearness of the mountains.

—Betty MacDonald, *The Egg and I*

LATE ONE WINTER DAY AS IT VERGED INTO early spring, I watched one of those quick-moving weather fronts that have the kind of fire in them that seems to need a special quality or state of atmosphere to set it off. The temperature had dropped to twenty degrees the night before. During the day, the wind blew strong from the southwest, beating against the rollers coming in from the open Atlantic and breaking on the outer shore, so that their great manes plumed up and sprayed away. By late afternoon the temperature had started to plummet again and the wind blew from the north, while fast-running clouds let down showers of snow and sleet.

The bay waters to the north were violently roughed up and studded with whitecaps. Waves tumbled, rocked, and splashed along the shore. Standing at a distance, I could see their white shapes heaving just above the far rims of the salt marsh, where the gulls seemed to be flinging across the sand dunes, making low arcs in their leaping. The grasses tossed and swayed, and they carried a fire on their blades which they caught from the sunset. The sun's western reaches were of a golden salmon color, of a metallic brilliance, making a deep, pure gash in the sky. Overland the running clouds were pink as flamingos, gray as a mole. The whole sky in its freezing beauty crossed all known boundaries, leaping like the gulls from one sea to another. This was light I was unable to catch or see, integral with a motion I could only conceive of, part of the incredible speed of planetary bodies, a beauty made of an infinity of variables. But it is of such furious unity that we, a feather, or a leaf are made, no matter how far we stray.

—John Hay, *The Undiscovered Country*

◆

FACTS OF THE

MATTER

"In winter nature is a cabinet of curiosities."

HENRY DAVID THOREAU

THE FIRST TIME I WENT IN SEARCH of the mountain goat I hiked into the Selway-Bitterroot Wilderness of western Montana. I had been told I might find the beast there. But the month was December, and the huge country around me was itself covered by a thick white coat. My telescope swung in futile arcs between snow mounds, gleaming crusts, chalk-colored rocks, weather-bleached snags, and icicles standing in dimly lit caves.

I made temporary camps away from the paths of snowslides to eat and rest. Otherwise my time was spent snowshoeing and scanning new sets of frozen cliffs and pinnacles, without success. After a good deal of searching I ended up with no more evidence than the early explorers to prove the creature a real one. No evidence, save perhaps distantly seen tracks which the wind and snow quickly covered.

Then one afternoon as I looked upward from a dark valley

bottom to where sunlight and clouds of fine ice crystals flared across a promontory, my binoculars caught the four-legged images I was after. They seemed, in a way, to be just that: images. Horned wraiths dissolving and reforming in swirls of drifting snow like figments of the imagination—mine, or maybe the mountains'.

I started up for a closer look, and it was slow, tense going. When I finally heaved up onto the ledge where I had seen the apparitions standing, they were gone. Tracks led to an ice-rimmed escarpment. My own hands and feet dug into the snow as I lay on my stomach and stretched forward to look where the prints of their feet disappeared into the airy gulf beyond.

I hugged my way around a corner to get out of the wind. Pausing to rub my nose and cheeks to chase the frost out of them, I became aware of two black horns and two liquid black eyes turning toward me. They hovered disembodied against the snow-filled sky and slopes. Behind the eyes a mound of snow began to shift, then erupted as the creature stood up from its bed and shook the last of the freshly fallen flakes from its back. Time passed—I don't recall how long—before the eyes and horns moved again and floated across a fissure. Suddenly, like a clot of tumbling snow, the beast bounded down a series of narrow ledges on a winter-slick wall of stone and was gone.

Where it had lain bedded, its body heat had melted a small impression. Wisps of fur were frozen to the ice in the bottom of it. I worked some strands loose and, somewhat like those scientists of an earlier day, rolled them between my fingers to assure myself that this was, after all, a flesh-and-blood animal.

—Douglas H. Chadwick, *A Beast the Color of Winter*

TOWARD THE END OF THIS STILL, piercingly cold winter's day, I crossed the snow-covered field beside the swamp and turned into a winding road. At every step, the snow squeaked shrilly beneath my feet. Distant sounds carried with startling distinctness. I heard the barking of a dog, an automobile engine starting, the mellow whistle of a locomotive far away. As I walked on, I fell to wondering about winter sounds.

Why do sounds seem to carry farther through cold air? Why do they reach the ear more distinctly in winter than in summer? I remember a farmer in Indiana who claimed he could guess where the mercury stood in the thermometer on clear midwinter days merely by listening to the sound of car wheels on a railroad track half a mile away beyond his pasture. The colder the day, the more distinctly every metallic rattle came to his ears. And why is it that snow squeaks loudest on the coldest days? I know the answer to these questions because I have just put them to a scientist friend of mine. Here are his explanations:

The squeaking of the snow is produced by sharp edges of

frozen crystals rubbing against each other. In mild weather, when the mercury stands just a little below freezing, the edges are less hard, more easily blunted. But as the mercury descends, the crystals become correspondingly harder, friction mounts and the high-pitched complaint of the rubbing corners and edges increases. "Snowball snow" that packs easily is squeakless. It is the harder crystals of the colder days that produce the shrill fifing of the snow beneath our feet.

The drop of mercury is also accompanied by the condensing of the atmosphere. When air is warmed, it expands and the molecules separate; when it is cooled, it contracts and the molecules draw closer together. This is the secret of far-carrying sounds on the winter air. The denser the medium, the better it transmits sound waves. If someone taps two stones together fifty feet away in the air, the sound is hardly noticeable. But if he does the same thing underwater, while you have your head beneath the surface, the sound is so penetrating it is painful. Water, denser than air, is a better conductor of sound. Steel rails are even better. Put your ear to a rail and you can catch sounds of an approaching train long before any noise reaches you by air.

If this is true, then why do we not hear sounds clearly in a blizzard when the density of the atmosphere is increased by falling flakes of snow? Instead, sounds are "blanketed" by snowfall. This is so, my friend explains, because the sound waves strike the solid matter of the flakes and are reflected back. The multitude of flakes in a blizzard cut out a large proportion of the waves. We hear only part of the sound, that part that passes between the falling flakes, and thus it reaches us in diminished volume.

— Edwin Way Teale, *Circle of the Seasons*

◆

L OOKING ACROSS THE WHITE FIELDS TODAY, I AM REMINDED
that an invariable rule of nature is that nothing is invariable.
"As like as two peas in a pod" is an exact statement of nature's ways.
For no two peas in a pod are ever exactly alike. Nature does not pla-
giarize herself, repeat herself. Her powers of innovation are bound-
less. No two hills or ants or oranges or sheep or snowflakes are identical. Ten thousand seem alike because we do not see them clearly
enough, because our senses are too dull or inadequate or inaccurate
to detect the differences.

And so it is with one of the oldest similes in the world: "As
white as the snow." The whiteness of the snow is infinitely varied.
In fact, its whiteness is produced by elements that are not white at
all. The individual crystals that go into the make-up of a snowflake
are transparent and colorless when they are created far up in the
sky. They are like clear glass. It is when they are grouped together in flakes, when they lie in untold millions in a drift, that they
appear white.

What is the explanation of this paradox? It is the same answer
that explains how a transparent window pane when it is broken and
powdered appears white while the intact pane is colorless. Both the
infinite number of crystals that make up the snowdrift and the vast
number of particles that comprise the powdered glass have so many

facets that they reflect all the rays of light in all directions. Put all the rays of the spectrum together and you have white just as when you take all the rays of the spectrum away you have black. It is the numberless crystals in the piled-up snow that turn it into a mound of the purest white.

Yet even this "purest white" has many subtle variations. The famous New York advertising photographer, H.I. Williams, once told me of his surprise in noting the difference in the whites recorded by his color camera. They all looked alike to his eyes. But the sensitive color film showed that some were tinged with blues or yellows or reds and some were pearly and opalescent. The white of a billiard ball, of a sheet of writing paper, or a dress shirt, or a tablecloth all were different. Probably no two tablecloths are exactly the same in whiteness, although our eyes are unable to detect the difference.

Similarly, it is likely that no two snowbanks are identical in the whiteness of their exterior. Their surroundings, the time of day, the conditions of the sky all contribute to their tinting. Even our eyes can note the blue in the shadows of trees stretching across the drifts and the pink glow of sunset spreading over an expanse of snow. But under the noonday sun, except when soot or mud has stained them or when old drifts have been discolored by deposits from the air, the whiteness of the snow remains all the same to our eyes—the purest white we know.

—Edwin Way Teale, *Circle of the Seasons*

SQUIRRELS BURY NUTS TO store food for winter, when there's little natural food. That's not news. What is interesting is that despite squirrels' intense interest in food, squirrels cannot remember where they've buried a nut for more than twenty minutes. Not very smart animals, after all, it seems. Or are they? Although squirrels don't know where their nuts are buried, they have no problem locating nuts that they or other squirrels have buried. Squirrels locate buried nuts using their sense of smell, and can find nuts buried under several inches of snow. In fact, most of the nuts a squirrel recovers will not be the ones it buried. Caching nuts is one of their most important survival instincts. Squirrels bury nuts communally so that all members of the species in the area benefit. Almost as soon as they leave the nest, young squirrels start burying nuts, although at first they don't completely cover the nut.

Squirrels can bury up to twenty-five nuts an hour. They bury nuts over a widely scattered area; this is called scatterhoarding.

There's another advantage to scatterhoarding besides providing nuts for other squirrels. There are many other species that forage for buried nuts, but if a competing species finds many nuts in a small area it will probably stay there. However, scatterhoarding, with its low density of nuts, prevents competitors from finding a large cache, because there is none.

Squirrels' burying instinct is powerful. In the building where I have my writing studio there's a woman who feeds squirrels on her windowsill. She mentioned that squirrels occasionally come into her apartment through the window. They steal peanuts from her kitchen counter and bury them in her avocado plant.

—Bill Adler, Jr., *Outwitting Squirrels*

IT GETS MIGHTY COLD ON THESE VERMONT winter nights. So cold, in fact, that an antiquated neighbor of mine — eighty years old if he's a day — says he's only forty. Claims he's been frozen solid half his life.

However, there's a limit. And as I stood in the snow on our nature trail contemplating an abandoned thrush's nest, I figured the limit had been passed. Although the trees crack and pop with the cold at thirty below, even an unprotected bird's nest isn't supposed to shiver. Yet that's just what this nest was doing. It shivered so hard that a powder of snow fell off its domed roof and sifted down in the moonlight.

In fact, what was a deserted bird's nest doing with a roof anyway? Perhaps it wasn't as empty as I'd thought. As I was about to investigate, something on the ground caught my eye. There in front of me was a clue, or rather a whole series of them: tiny, lacy footprints. They ran in lines over the snow, etched in moonlight and shadow, and showing the drag mark of a long, slender tail. I was in the presence of white-footed mouse, one of the many creatures who leave their stories in the snow.

A confirmed tree climber, the deer mouse, as it is often called, totes milkweed fuzz, feathers from a bird carcass, or even the stuffing from a mattress to remodel some bird's summer home. There it can be out of harm's way.

Like many other creatures, the deer mouse shows its habits by its tracks. Its bounding gait, like an animated rubber ball, brings its hind feet in front of its forefeet so that the hind tracks register ahead of the smaller front ones. And like most tree dwellers, such as the squirrels, the tracks of its forefeet are paired with each other instead of being placed diagonally as are the tracks of rabbits and ground-dwelling field mice.

If you learn to identify a few tracks of the common animals you can be in on the start of a whole Winter Whodunit. Tracks and other signs speak volumes about the creature that made them. In fact, what we often call "the dead of winter" can be a fascinating time for animal study. Wherever a living creature goes it leaves a record.

—Ronald Rood, *Wild Brother*

A Unique Creation

I N ITS MICROSCOPIC FORMS, SNOW EPITOMIZES ETHEREAL
beauty. It is a cliché to say that no two snowflakes are identical,
but it is a fact that each single snowflake that has fallen throughout
all of time, and that will fall throughout what remains of time, has
been — will be — a unique creation in symmetry and form.

I know of one man who has devoted most of his adult life to
the study of this transient miracle. He has built a special house fitted
with a freezing system, instead of heating equipment. It is a house
with a gaping hole in its roof. On snowy days and nights he sits in icy
solitude catching the falling flakes on plates of pre-chilled glass and
hurriedly photographing them through an enlarging lens. For him the
fifth elemental in its infinite diversity and singularity is beauty incar-
nate, and a thing to worship.

—Farley Mowat, *The Northern Territories*

THRILLS

AND CHILLS

"The vitality of thought is in adventure."

ALFRED NORTH WHITEHEAD

◆

ONE OF THE MOST BEAUTIful and exhilarating storms I ever enjoyed in the Sierra occurred in December, 1874, when I happened to be exploring one of the tributary valleys of the Yuba River. The day was intensely pure, one of those incomparable bits of California winter, warm and balmy and full of white sparkling sunshine, redolent of all the purest influences of the spring, and at the same time enlivened with one of the most bracing wind-storms conceivable.

When the storm began to sound, I lost no time in pushing out into the woods to enjoy it. For on such occasions Nature has always something rare to show us, and the danger to life and limb is hardly greater than one would experience crouching deprecatingly beneath a roof.

Toward midday, after a long, tingling scramble through copses of hazel and ceanothus, I gained the summit of the highest ridge in the neighborhood; and then it occurred to me that it would be a fine thing to climb one of the trees to obtain a wider outlook and get my ear close to the Aeolian music of its topmost needles. After cautiously casting about, I made choice of the tallest of a group of Douglas Spruces that were growing close together like a tuft of grass, no one of which seemed likely to fall unless all the rest fell with it. Though comparatively young, they were about 100 feet high, and their lithe, brushy tops were rocking and swirling in wild ecstasy. Being accustomed to climb trees in making botanical studies, I experienced no difficulty in reaching the top of this one, and never before did I enjoy so noble an exhilaration of motion. The slender tops fairly flapped and swished in the passionate torrent, bending and swirling backward and forward, round and round, tracing indescribable combinations of vertical and horizontal curves, while I clung with muscles firm braced, like a bobolink on a reed.

In its widest sweeps my tree-top described an arc of from twenty to thirty degrees, but I felt sure of its elastic temper, having seen others of the same species still more severely tried—bent almost to the ground indeed, in heavy snows—without breaking a fiber. I was therefore safe, and free to take the wind into my pulses and enjoy the excited forest from my superb outlook.

The sounds of the storm corresponded gloriously with [a] wild exuberance of light and motion. The profound bass of the naked branches and boles booming like waterfalls; the quick, tense vibrations of the pine-needles, now rising to a shrill, whistling hiss, now falling to a silky murmur; the rustling of laurel groves in the dells, and the keen metallic click of leaf on leaf—all this was heard in easy analysis when the attention was calmly bent.

I kept my lofty perch for hours, frequently closing my eyes to enjoy the music by itself, or to feast quietly on the delicious fragrance that was streaming past. The fragrance of the woods was less marked than that produced during warm rain, when so many balsamic buds and leaves are steeped like tea; but, from the chafing of resiny branches against each other, and the incessant attrition of myriads of needles, the gale was spiced to a very tonic degree.

We all travel the milky way together, trees and men; but it never occurred to me until this stormday, while swinging in the wind, that trees are travelers, in the ordinary sense. They make many journeys, not extensive ones, it is true; but our own little journeys, away and back again, are only little more than tree-wavings— many of them not so much.

When the storm began to abate, I dismounted and sauntered down through the calming woods. The storm-tones died away, and, turning toward the east, I beheld the countless hosts of the forests hushed and tranquil, towering above one another on the slopes of the hills like a devout audience. The setting sun filled them with amber light, and seemed to say, while they listened, "My peace I give unto you."

As I gazed on the impressive scene, all the so-called ruin of the storm was forgotten, and never before did these noble woods appear so fresh, so joyous, so immortal.

—John Muir, *The Mountains of California*

THE SOUND BEGAN AS A LOW ROAR FAR UP THE CANYON. THEN it shrieked, groaned, and tore its way out of the sky as if a giant object were falling. Powerless, we braced ourselves for the inevitable shock. Out of the darkness it came: the headlong, invisible charge of the wind. Our tent leaned, twisted, stretched, and flapped, until it seemed no longer anchored to the ground. Then, suddenly, all was still again, except for the whisper of the falling snow and the anxious, uneven breathing of the four men inside the tiny shelter.

For four days and five nights we sat out the biggest winter storm of 1974 in our camp at 10,000 feet in the White Mountains of California. Winds of more than one hundred miles per hour, we learned later, had ripped the ice from the surface of a large lake twenty miles to the west. During a lull near the end of the storm, we skied to a grove of lodgepole pines in search of wood for a warming and drying fire. We found a healthy tree more than two feet in diameter that had been freshly broken—snapped off ten feet above the base. The broken piece, which must have weighed tons, had been carried thirty feet by the wind without leaving a single mark in the snow.

The four of us were attempting the first winter traverse of the eighty-mile-long crest of the White Mountains. Paralleling the Sierra

on the east side of the Owens Valley, these arid mountains have few trees, no lakes, very few fishing streams, and a Great Basin climate, with recorded temperatures reaching as low as −38° F. Pellisier Flats, an eight-mile-long plateau at 13,000 feet, freezes every month of the year and has real arctic tundra. The crest of the range averages over 12,000 feet. Miles of treeless highlands are exposed to relentless west winds.

[When the storm abated] we were off again onto snow that squeaked underfoot. For miles we followed treeless highlands, imperceptibly descending a thousand feet toward a gentle meeting with timberline. Not far from here a friend of mine had sat around a fire with a scientist named Edmund Schulman on a cool September evening in the 1950s. As the two men warmed their hands, Schulman pulled a brand from the fire and examined it closely. "1277 to 1283 A.D.," my friend recalls him saying. "This six-year ring pattern never repeats itself." When he had finished studying the flame-blackened ring pattern, he tossed the wood back into the fire. It burned long and hot and even.

Schulman had visited the bristlecones when the snow was gone and the trees rose naked from rocky ground. We saw them in quite a different setting, approaching on skis through an open forest clothed in white. The Patriarch Grove resembled a giant stage occupied by a troupe of frozen dancers; each tree seemed involved in the same motion, caught in pirouette, limbs extended. The west wind had shaped them and coated them with fingers of ice. They seemed to point toward some distant force in the sky.

We camped on the edge of the grove, watching sunrise color ancient bristlecone limbs while a full moon touched the horizon of the distant Sierra. It seemed a sacrilege even to hang our sleeping bags to dry on those trees. Each of us ran his hands over their wood, feeling the sensual warmth of a living thing that was already old in the winters of 1492 and 1776. Compared to these trees, we were a renewable resource.

—Galen Rowell, *High and Wild*

I TRAVERSED IN BOATS THIS SAME canyon several times. Once in the winter of 1897-98, the most severe known in Utah and Arizona for many years; when, in places, the River was frozen over in the quiet portions in Glen Canyon, and I went from Dandy Crossing to Lee's Ferry with my friend John Ginty and his son, of San Francisco, and a couple of men, where, for miles, we had to cut our way through the ice with axes. The ice was thick enough for us to walk and skid our boats upon. At places, the whole mass would be moving down the River while we were cutting our way through it, and, coming out at the head of the rapid, we would be carried through, surrounded by huge cakes of ice that were broken off the advancing sheet at the head of the rapid. Such an experience, in some of the heavier, low-water rapids of Glen Canyon, was more nervous work and more dangerous than running many of the rapids of the Grand Canyon, for, going through the rapids, even though their waves were only three or four feet high, surrounded by cakes of ice, surging, swaying, grinding and crushing against the boat, we were entirely at the mercy of the current and the ice, as we could neither row nor steer. Fortunately, by using poles with spikes in their ends, pushing against the ice and the cliffs as we went by, we reached Lee's Ferry in safety, and had the pleasure of a nine days' tramp to the railroad, sleeping out in the snow every night, without tents or other shelter than our blankets, while the thermometer ranged from 10 to 30 degrees below zero.

> —John Wesley Powell,
>
> *Exploration of the Colorado River and its Tributaries*

FEW YOSEMITE VISITORS EVER SEE SNOW avalanches and fewer still know the exhilaration of riding on them. In all my mountaineering I have enjoyed only one avalanche ride, and the start was so sudden and the end came so soon I had but little time to think of the danger that attends this sort of travel, though at such times one thinks fast. One fine Yosemite morning after a heavy snowfall, being eager to see as many avalanches as possible and wide views of the forest and summit peaks in their new white robes before the sunshine had time to change them, I set out early to climb by a side cañon to the top of a commanding ridge a little over three thousand feet above the Valley. On account of the looseness of the snow that blocked the cañon I knew the climb would require a long time, some three or four hours as I estimated; but it proved far more difficult than I had anticipated. Most of the way I sank waist deep, almost out of sight in some places. After spending the whole day to within half an hour or so of sundown, I was still several hundred feet below the summit. Then my hopes were reduced to getting up in time to see the sunset. But I was not to get summit views of any sort that day, for deep trampling near the cañon head, where the snow was strained, started an avalanche, and I was swished down to the foot of the cañon as if by enchantment. The wallowing ascent had taken nearly all day, the descent only about a minute. When the avalanche started I threw myself on my back and spread my arms to try to keep from sinking. Fortunately, though the grade of cañon is very steep, it is not interrupted by precipices large enough to cause outbounding or free plunging. On no part of the rush was I buried. I was only moderately imbedded on the surface or at times a little below it, and covered with a veil of back-streaming dust particles; and as the whole mass beneath and about me joined in the flight there was no friction, though I was tossed here and there and lurched from side to side. When the avalanche swedged and came to rest I found myself on top of the crumpled pile without a bruise or scar. This was a fine experience. Hawthorne says somewhere that steam has spiritualized travel; though unspiritual smells, smoke, etc., still attend steam travel. This flight in what might be called a milky way of snow-stars was the most spiritual and exhilarating of all the modes of motion I have ever experienced. Elijah's flight in a chariot of fire could hardly have been more gloriously exciting.

—John Muir, *The Yosemite*

CREATURES OF THE
WINTER WILD

"What is life?
It is the flash of a firefly in the night.
It is the breath of a buffalo in the wintertime."

CROWFOOT, BLACKFOOT WARRIOR

◆

Coyote Song

THE COYOTES ARE SINGING ALMOST every night now down in the hollow, the creek bed that runs below my southern boundary. Their song is a chorus of yips, yelps and barks that increases in intensity and number as more and more join in, until it climaxes in a series of howled wails. I hear them year around occasionally down there or over by the river, but it is their breeding season now and they are singing more often.

I like lying in bed as I did last night, with moonlight streaming in the window, listening to their song. Coyote. That name comes from the Aztec's word for them, *coyotl,* and should, to my way of thinking, always be pronounced ki-o-tee, not ki-oat, the way it sometimes is. Coy-o-tee, that word handed down from long ago, a clumsy approximation of their song, the song of wild things in the moonlight.

—Sue Hubbell, *A Country Year*

ALL WINTER LONG, IN THE LATE DUSK AND SOMETIMES UNTIL dawn, the foxes hunt. They patter silently through the deep drifted snow on their little dog feet, sniffing with lean uplifted muzzles for the scent of a partridge, pawing in search of tunneling deermice. Their hunting is not easy in the winter months, and the whole of their energy is given over to it. A fox is solitary, mateless, in the winter season. He maintains no home to which to return when he has filled his belly, but sleeps away the daylight hours wherever he can find a sheltered place, under a thickneedled pine or in the lee of a fallen log, or wherever he can dig out a form in the powdery snow. He sleeps as an Eskimo dog does, curled up, his heavy-furred tail brush wrapped across his feet and nose so that he breathes through the fur. The ingredients of his winter days are only sleeping exhaustedly and prowling forth again for food.

—Alan Devoe, *Lives Around Us*

ANIMAL NOISES ARE RARE IN the deep of winter. On occasion I have heard the sharp bark of a fox, maybe on a hunt, maybe challenging some comfort-loving dog to a game of chase through the deep snows of the back-hill woods. Once, and only once, I heard the death scream of a rabbit caught by a fox or an owl. I do not think I want to hear it again. It is the most blood-curdling scream I have ever heard, although I must admit to limited experience along this line. It sounds both human and inhuman at one and the same time, the shrill, agonizing shriek of a lost soul bound to perdition. No, I am sure I never want to hear it again.

The most frequently heard animal sounds of winter nights, however, are the calls of owls. This is not to say that they are heard so frequently as to be commonplace, but I suspect we sleep through a great many performances. There are great horned owls in other parts of town, but we have never heard them around our house. Barred owls are not uncommon, and their hooting is unmistakable: "hoohoo, hoohoo . . . hoohoo, hoohoo-aw," two distinct groups of four hoots each. Hence, one of its other names, Eight-Hooter.

But by far the most common of the tribe is the little screech owl, a misnomer if there ever was one. Records of people who have actually heard this bird screech are almost non-existent. In fact, the only one I have come across was when Forbush and Brewster, a couple of top-flight field observers, heard a sound like "the first notes of a siren whistle," and when it seemingly changed to the familiar call of a screech owl, decided that was it. They never saw the bird.

—Henry B. Kane, *A Care for Nature*

CRICKETS CHIRP A LOT. THAT JUST ABOUT covers the subject of Crickets except for a few minor details. The House Cricket, or Cricket on the Hearth, starts chirping at dusk and chirps all night. That makes it nice for the people who live there, for Crickets sound so cheerful and cozy. Some people can't get to sleep unless they hear Crickets chirping. They will bring Crickets in from the country and turn them loose on the hearth. Sometimes I think I don't understand life at all.[1] Field Crickets chirp in the daytime too. They often move into the house when the weather is cool.[2] Field Crickets eat woollen and linen goods, but only when they are hungry. Some people begrudge them even a small piece out of a suit of clothes. Have Crickets no rights? The Snowy Tree Cricket, or Temperature Cricket, is the most useful kind. According to Edwin Way Teale, the Snowy Cricket's rate of chirping varies with the weather so exactly that you can find the temperature in Fahrenheit degrees by dividing the number of chirps per minute by four and adding forty.[3] If you have a thermometer but no Cricket, multiplying the degrees of Fahrenheit by four and subtracting one hundred and sixty gives you the number of times the Snowy Tree Cricket would have chirped per minute if you had one. The thermometer offers you more for your money.[4] It does the work of both and you don't have to climb a tree to get at it. Only the male Cricket chirps. He does it by rubbing his tegmina, or front wings, together, thus throwing the tympana of the tegmina into rapid vibration.[5] Scientists now tell us that the Cricket is not chirping a love song to his mate, as most of us have always believed. They say he chirps just to be chirping and that he is not a bit romantic. The fact remains that when you find one Cricket under a piece of old newspaper you always find two. But I'm not going to argue about it. I don't care enough.

—Will Cuppy, *How to Become Extinct*

---

[1] Lettuce leaves, apple cores, moist bread and bone meal scattered around the floor at bedtime will make them chirp louder and longer.

[2] Crickets would rather be warm than almost anything else. I'm the same way myself.

[3] A few Crickets chirp faster or slower than they really should. Can Professor Teale help it if you try the wrong Cricket?

[4] The Snowy Tree Cricket cannot tell you what day of the week it is. He doesn't know.

[5] Crickets have their ears on their front legs. Nothing surprises me any more.

◆

A FLOCK OF A DOZEN CHICKADEES SPENDS THE YEAR IN MY woods. In winter, when we are harvesting diseased or dead trees for our fuel wood, the ring of the axe is dinner gong for the chickadee tribe. They hang in the offing waiting for the tree to fall, offering pert commentary on the slowness of our labor. When the tree at last is down, and the wedges begin to open up its contents, the chickadees draw up their white napkins and fall to. Every slab of dead bark is, to them, a treasury of eggs, larvae, and cocoons. For them every ant-tunneled heartwood bulges with milk and honey. We often stand in a fresh split against a nearby tree just to see the greedy chicks mop up the ant-eggs. It lightens our labor to know that they, as well as we, derive aid and comfort from the fragrant riches of newly split oak.

— Aldo Leopold, *Sand County Almanac*

The Long Sleep

I NDIANS SPOKE OF HIBERNATION AS THE LONG SLEEP, BUT IT is rather more than that. It is profound oblivion midway between sleep and death. It is an unknowing and unfeeling more deep and lasting than can be induced in man by the most powerful drugs, a suspension of life processes more thorough and protracted than even the "frozen slumber" which doctors have lately devised as a palliative of cancer. It is a phenomenon unique in nature, and though we are wiser about it than we were in those cradle-days of biology when Dr. Johnson thought that swallows passed the winter asleep in the mud at the bottom of the Thames, it remains a riddle still.

Most striking is the Long Sleep of the mammals. Raccoons, chipmunks, bats, bears, woodchucks—all these make ready in autumn for a greater or lesser period of dormancy. They are all animals with imprecisely regulated body temperatures, these mammalian hibernators; during normal summer-time activity their temperatures often fluctuate by ten or fifteen degrees. They do not have a wholly static temperature, independent of the warmth of the outer air, as does a man or a wood-mouse or a winter-active deer. They can survive the months of northern cold and snow only by lapsing into a quiescence hardly distinguishable from death. Some of them sleep more deeply than others, some for the whole winter and some for only a part of it. The commonest of them, the woodchuck, serves as a fair exemplar.

The woodchuck's hibernation usually starts about the middle of September. For weeks he has been foraging with increased appetite among the clover blossoms and has grown heavy and slow-moving. Now, with the coming of mid-September, apples and corn and yarrow-tops have become less plentiful, and the nights are cool. The woodchuck moves with slower gait, and emerges less and less frequently for feeding-trips. Layers of fat have accumulated around his chest and shoulders, and there is thick fat in the axils of his legs. He has extended his summer burrow to a length of nearly thirty feet, and has fashioned a deep nest-chamber at the end of it, far below the level of the frost. He has carried in, usually, a little hay. He is ready for the Long Sleep.

When the temperature of the September days falls below 50 degrees or so, the woodchuck becomes too drowsy to come forth from his burrow in the chilly dusk to forage. He remains in the deep nest-chamber, lethargic, hardly moving. Gradually, with the passing of hours or days, his coarse-furred body curls into a semi-circle, like a foetus, nose-tip touching tail. The small legs are tucked in, the hand-like clawed forefeet folded. The woodchuck has become a compact ball. Presently the temperature of his body begins to fall.

In normal life the woodchuck's temperature, though fluctuant, averages about 97 degrees. Now, as he lies tight-curled in a ball with the winter sleep stealing over him, this body heat drops ten degrees,

twenty degrees, thirty. Finally, by the time the snow is on the ground and the woodchuck's winter dormancy has become complete, his temperature is only 38 or 40. With the falling of the body heat there is a slowing of his heartbeat and his respiration. In normal life he breathes thirty or forty times each minute; when he is excited, as many as a hundred times. Now he breathes slower and slower — ten times a minute, five times a minute, once a minute, and at last only ten or twelve times in an hour. His heartbeat is a twentieth of normal. He has entered fully into the oblivion of hibernation.

The Long Sleep lasts, on an average, about six months. For half a year the woodchuck remains unmoving, hardly breathing. His pituitary gland is inactive; his blood is so sluggishly circulated that there is an unequal distribution in the chilled body; his sensory awareness has wholly ceased. It is almost true to say that he has altered from a warm-blooded to a cold-blooded animal.

Then, in the middle of March, he wakes. The waking is not a slow and gradual thing, as was the drifting into sleep, but takes place quickly, often in an hour. The body temperature ascends to normal, or rather higher for a while; glandular functions instantly resume; the respiration quickens and steadies at a normal rate. The woodchuck has become himself again, save only that he is a little thinner, and is ready at once to fare forth into the pale spring sunlight and look for grass and berries.

Such is the performance each fall and winter, with varying detail, of bats and worms and bears, and a hundred other kinds of creature. It is a marvel less spectacular than the migration flight of hummingbirds or the flash of shooting stars, but is not much less remarkable.

—Alan Devoe, *Lives Around Us*

◆

BY THE MORNING OF THE LAST day, the pond was graven in the final shape of this absolute season. The wind died, and light snow fell from a lowering sky. Against this was fixed the eternally wheeling bird. But it was not the red-tailed hawk. It was a raven. He had survived with equanimity the changing seasons and the death of his solitary yearling, killed by a weasel, and the disappearance of his mate. He had come to the pond and marsh as was his custom and looked down on them for the thirteenth season in his life.

He had watched the withdrawal of life from the north and had flown with some of the southward-streaming ducks. He had seen salamanders swimming up streams and toads jumping through woodlands and a profusion of life pouring past him to the south. He had impassively watched the arrival of the northern buntings and finches and a pair of arctic owls with whom he would have to share some of the hunting at the pond.

The raven was one of the great watchers. His long experience was preserved in a fund of memories that made him wilier and more watchful the older he grew. Now that the year of the pond was fading into the past, he personified that year and the others before it.

In [his] memory was every detail of the spring awakening: the reaching for space, light, expression; the languorous heat of summer days; the slow waning metabolism of the last season; and the long sleep away from the sun. In every speck of living matter, there was this memory of the indestructible life force of earth.

The raven turned into northern haze and disappeared; the sleepers slept on; and the pond moved to infinity.

— Franklin Russell, *Watchers at the Pond*

A c k n o w l e d g m e n t s

"Winter's Spectrum" by Hal Borland, from *Borland Country,* by Hal Borland, published by J.B. Lippincott Company. Copyright © 1971 by Barbara Dodge Borland, as executor of the estate of Hal Borland. Reprinted by permission of Frances Collin, Literary Agent.

"Night Lights" by Helen Hoover, from *The Long-Shadowed Forest* by Helen Hoover, published by W. W. Norton & Company, Inc. Copyright © 1972 by Helen Hoover and Adrian Hoover. Reprinted by permission of the publisher.

"Grand Canyon Dawn" by John Wesley Powell, from "Exploration of the Colorado River and Its Tributaries" by John Wesley Powell. From *Down the Colorado,* by Robert Brewster Stanton, edited and with an Introduction by Dwight L. Smith, published by the University of Oklahoma Press. Copyright © 1965 by the University of Oklahoma Press. Reprinted by permission of the publisher.

"The Muskrat Pool" by Alan Devoe, with Mary Berry Devoe, from *Our Animal Neighbors* by Alan Devoe, with Mary Berry Devoe, published by McGraw-Hill, Inc. Copyright © 1953 by Alan and Mary Berry Devoe. Reprinted by permission of the publisher.

"December Moon" by Hal Borland, from *Twelve Moons of the Year* by Hal Borland, edited by Barbara Dodge Borland, published by Alfred A. Knopf. Copyright © 1979 by Barbara Dodge Borland, as executor of the estate of Hal Borland. Reprinted by permission of Frances Collin, Literary Agent.

"Winter Prophets" by Ronald Rood, from *Who Wakes the Groundhog?* by Ronald Rood, published by W. W. Norton & Company, Inc. Copyright © 1973 by Ronald Rood. Reprinted by permission of the author and publisher.

"Let's Talk About the Weather" and "Winter Reveals" by Annie Dillard. Excerpts from *Pilgrim at Tinker Creek* by Annie Dillard, published by Harper & Row, Publishers, Inc. Copyright © 1974 by Annie Dillard. Reprinted by permission of the publisher.

◆